The Jackson Family

of

Woore and Wirral

By Colin Jackson

First published 2011
Reprinted 2015

ISBN: 978-1514685655   © 2011 Colin Jackson / Mercianotes

Contact the author: colin.jackson@mercianotes.com
Contact the publisher: enquiries@mercianotes.com

Published jointly by:
Mercianotes   CreateSpace
Wigton   Charlrston,SC,
CA7 5AQ   USA
United Kingdom

Contents

Conventions used in this book

♀	Female.
♂	Male
?	unknown date
Year?	approximate date

Notes on Pedigree One
Edward Jackson 1740 - 1807

The Parents

1♂ Edward Jackson was born in about 1740. 1770: Edward married Esther of whom nothing is known. 27 Nov. 1807: He died in Woore, Shropshire and buried in Woore Chapel.

The Children

2♂ George Jackson was born 1770 in Woore, 15 Jul 1770: Christened in Woore Chapel. 28 Dec 1808: Married Hannah Brereton in St Mary's, Muckleston, witnessed by Richard Skellorn and Ann Brereton.
1841 Census: Aged 65. (71?) Living in Woore with his Wife Hannah (66) and three Granddaughters, Jane Jackson (8) Martha Jackson (7) and Mary Ann Jackson (5)
1851 Census: Aged 81 Living in Woore with his Wife Hannah aged 76, Mary his daughter aged 35, a dress-maker, his Son Samuel aged 30, a blacksmith, and his two grand-daughters, Martha aged 17 and Mary Ann aged 15.
1856: He was a Blacksmith in Woore, he died aged 85 of senility.
1 Jan 1856: He was buried in St Mary's, Muckleston, Staffordshire.

2a♀ Hannah Brereton daughter of Samuel Brereton and Han Wilkison [Ann Wilkinson]. 1776: Hannah was born in Aston, Shropshire. 21 Jul 1776: She was christened in St Mary's, Muckleston.
1841-1851 see census details above.
9 Sep 1852: Hannah died in Woore (aged 76) of Bronchitis.

3♂ William Jackson was born in 1779 in Woore. 17 Nov 1771: christened in the Chapel. Woore.

4♀ Mary Jackson died in 1779 in Woore. 12 Dec 1779: She was buried in Woore Chapel.

The Grandchildren

5♂ William Jackson was born in 1809 in Woore. Full details are given in Pedigree 2

6♂ George Jackson was born in 1810 in Woore. Full details are given in Pedigree 4.

7♂ Edward Jackson was born in 1812 in Woore. Full details are given in Pedigree 5.

8♀ Mary Jackson was born in 1814 in Woore. 12 Jun 1814: She was christened in St. Mary's, Muckleston.
Mary married Mr. Sneyd.

9♀ Martha Jackson was born in 1817 in Woore. 9 Feb 1817: She was christened in St. Mary's, Muckleston.

10♂ John James Jackson was born in 1818 in Woore, Shropshire and was christened in Muckleston Parish Church, Staffordshire.
John married Mary Hilditch.

3o♀ Ann Jackson daughter of John James Jackson and Mary Hilditch was born on 10 Feb 1848 in Woore.

10a♀ Mary Hilditch was born in 1824 in Muckleston.

11♂ Samuel Jackson was born in 1819 in Full details are given in Pedigree 6.

Woore and Muckleston

The Italian-style church of the Shropshire village of Woore whose belfry has a public address system instead of the traditional bells, stands testimony of this newly defined parish. Although the village itself is mentioned in the Domesday Book, its religious base was the nearby Staffordshire village of Muckleston. Many people who are recorded in the Muckleston Parish Register were resident in Woore. Indeed, in the 1960's some Woore residents were buried in Muckleston alongside their forebears.

The parent church in Muckleston provided a chapel of ease in Woore, which was located in the grounds of the current vicarage. Old documents refer to this Woore Chapel that should not be confused with the Methodist Chapel, which is a more recent building.

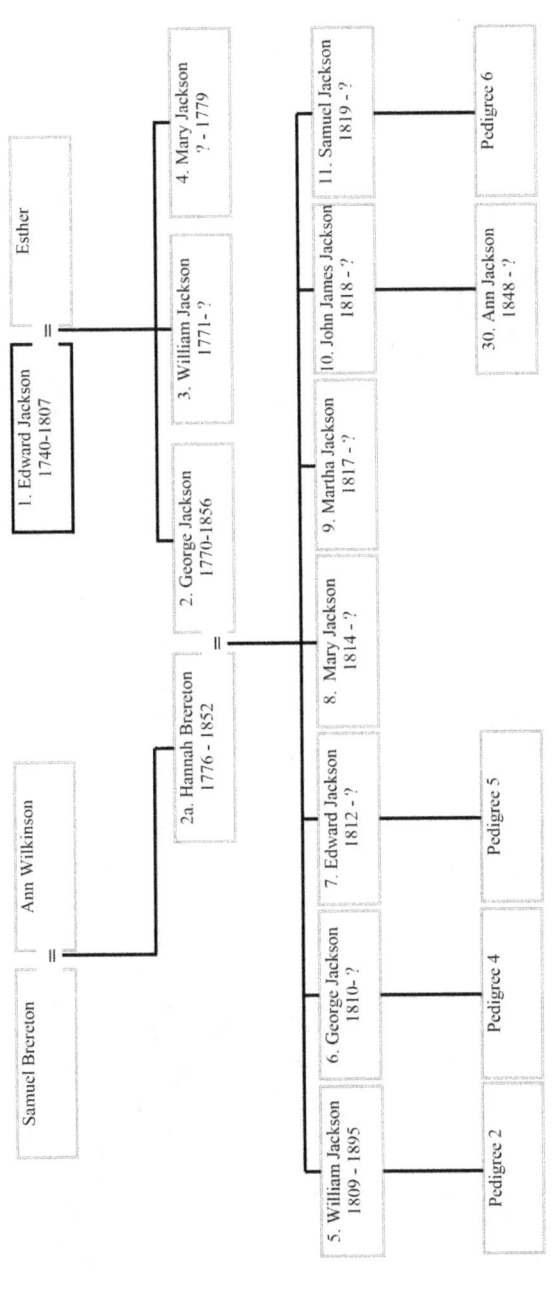

Pedigree One
Edward Jackson 1740 - 1807

Samuel Brereton

Ann Wilkinson

Esther

1. Edward Jackson
1740-1807

2a. Hannah Brereton
1776 - 1852

4. Mary Jackson
? - 1779

3. William Jackson
1771- ?

2. George Jackson
1770-1856

11. Samuel Jackson
1819 - ?

10. John James Jackson
1818 - ?

9. Martha Jackson
1817 - ?

8. Mary Jackson
1814 - ?

7. Edward Jackson
1812 - ?

6. George Jackson
1810- ?

5. William Jackson
1809 - 1895

30. Ann Jackson
1848 - ?

Pedigree 6

Pedigree 5

Pedigree 4

Pedigree 2

Notes on Pedigree Two Alpha
William Jackson 1809-1895
And Jemima 1805 - 1837

The Parents

5♂

William Jackson was born in 1809 in Woore, Shropshire, the son of a blacksmith.

5 Jul 1809: He was christened in St Mary's, Muckleston, Staffordshire.

1830: William married Jemima.

1840: William traveled to Birkenhead with his Brother Samuel, presumably looking for work at the newly opened Cammel Lairds Shipyards.

1841 Census: Aged 32. Living in the home of Samuel Simpson and his wife Mary in Overchurch in the Parish of Upton. William was with his brother Samuel, both Blacksmiths.

6 June 1843: William married Mary Smith in St Nicholas, Liverpool.

1851 Census: Aged 42. living with his wife, Mary Smith aged 28, and his four children, John, George, Henry and Ann, ages 8, 6, 4, 2, at The Pastures, close to Primrose Hill, New Ferry. He was a blacksmith.

1861 Census: Aged 52. living with his wife, Mary, aged 39, and eight children. John 18, George 16, Henry 14, Ann 12, Margaret 10, Martha 5, William 7, Thomas 3 months at 6 Olinda Street. New Ferry. He was a blacksmith.

1871 Census: Aged 62, living with Mary, 19, and George 26, Henry 24, William 17, Isaac 10, Elizabeth 7, at 6 Olinda Street. New Ferry. He was a smith.

1881 Census: Aged 72. Living with Mary, 60, and Isaac 20, at 6 Olinda Street. New Ferry. He was a blacksmith.

1891 Census: Aged 82. Living with Mary.

25 Dec 1895: He died in Bebington, Cheshire and was buried in St. Andrew's Church Yard, Bebington.

5a♀

Jemima was William's first wife.

1805: born in Market Drayton

1830: married William

1837: She died in Woore aged 32 of consumption (tuberculosis).

William's second wife, Mary Smith, and their children are described in Pedigree Two Beta.

The Children of William and Jemima

21♀

Martha Jackson was born in 1831 in Woore.

17 Aug 1831: She was christened in St Mary's, Muckleston.

1841 Census: Aged 7. Living in Woore with her grandparents George and Hannah.

1851 Census: Aged 17 living in Woore with her grandparents George and Hannah.

22♀

Mary Ann Jackson was born in 1836 in Woore, Shropshire. Full details on Pedigree 3.

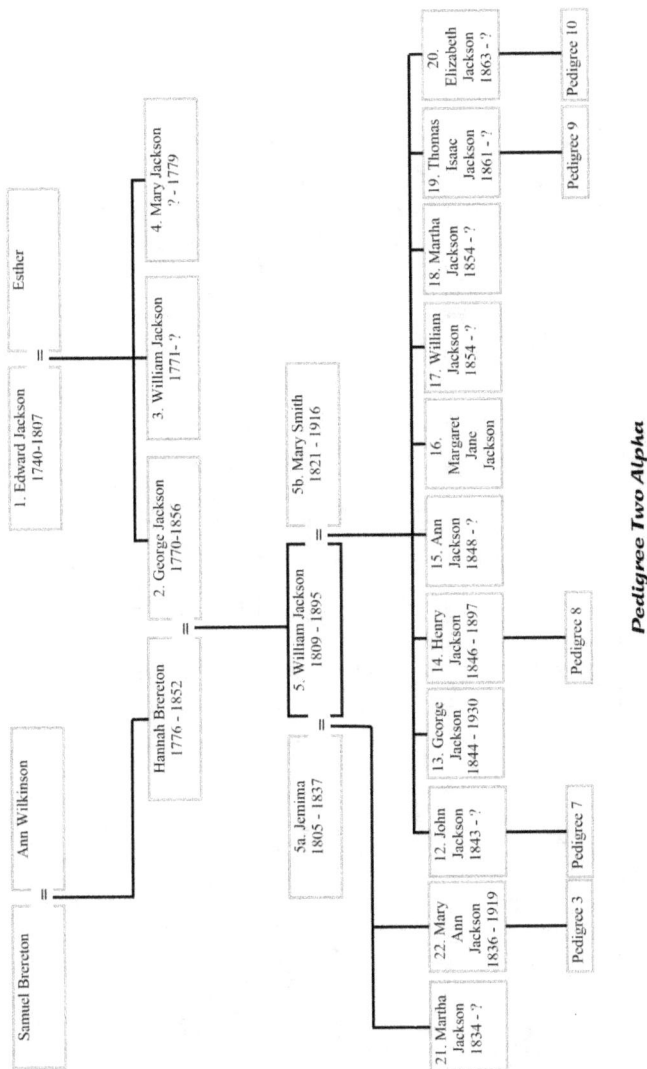

Pedigree Two Alpha
William Jackson 1809-1895
And Jemima 1805 - 1837

Samuel Brereton

Ann Wilkinson

Edward Jackson
1740-1807

Esther

Hannah Brereton
1776 - 1852

2. George Jackson
1770-1856

3. William Jackson
1771-?

4. Mary Jackson
? - 1779

5. William Jackson
1809 - 1895

5a. Jemima
1805 - 1837

5b. Mary Smith
1821 - 1916

21. Martha
Jackson
1834 - ?

22. Mary
Ann
Jackson
1836 - 1919

12. John
Jackson
1843 - ?

13. George
Jackson
1844 - 1930

14. Henry
Jackson
1846 - 1897

15. Ann
Jackson
1848 - ?

16.
Margaret
Jane
Jackson

17. William
Jackson
1854 - ?

18. Martha
Jackson
1854 - ?

19. Thomas
Isaac
Jackson
1861 - ?

20.
Elizabeth
Jackson
1863 - ?

Pedigree 3

Pedigree 7

Pedigree 8

Pedigree 9

Pedigree 10

Notes on Pedigree Two Beta
William Jackson 1809-1895
And Mary (Smith) 1821 - 1916

The Parents

5♂ William Jackson was born in 1809 in Woore, Shropshire, the Son of a Blacksmith.

William's life is described in Pedigree Two Alpha with details of his first wife and their children.

5♀ Mary Smith was William's second wife. Mary was the Daughter of John and Nancy Smith a Farmer of 30 acres, of Saughall Massey, Moreton, Wirral.

6 Jul 1821: Mary was born in Saughall, Upton, Cheshire.

7 Oct 1821: She was christened in St Oswald's, Bidston, Cheshire.

6 June 1843: married William in St Nicholas's, Liverpool.

1851 Census: Aged 28, living with William, and their 1 children, at The Pastures, close to Primrose Hill New ferry

1861 Census: Aged 39, living with William, and their 8 Children, at 6 Olinda Street, New Ferry.

1871 Census: Aged 49 living with William, and their Children, at Olinda Street, New Ferry.

1881 Census: Aged 60 living with William, and their son Isaac, at 6 Olinda Street, New ferry

1891 Census: living with William.

1895 William died

11 Mar 1916: She died in New Ferry, and was buried in St Andrew's Church Yard, Bebington.

The Children of William and Mary

12♂ John Jackson was born in 1843 in Carr, Moreton, Cheshire. Full details on Pedigree 7.

13♂ George Jackson was born on 23 Sep 1844 in Carr, Moreton, Cheshire.

3 Nov 1844: He was christened in St. Oswald's Church, Bidston.

1851 Census: Aged 6, living with his parents at The Pastures, close to Primrose Hill New ferry.

1861 Census: Aged 16, living with his parents at 6 Olinda Street, New Ferry

1871 Census: Aged 26, living with his parents at 6 Olinda Street, New Ferry

10 Apr 1871: married Louisa Morecroft in St Andrews, Bebington.

1886 Louisa died

11 Apr 1887: George married Marcy Evans in St Paul's, Rock Ferry, Cheshire

18 Dec 1930: George died in 10 Grove St. New Ferry, Cheshire. He was a general labourer. He was buried in St Andrew's, Bebington.

13a♀ Louisa Morecroft, was George's first wife. She was the daughter of George Morecroft. Louisa was born about 1850.

13b♀ Marcy Evans was George Jackson's second wife.

14♂ Henry Jackson was born on 17 Dec 1846 in Carr, Moreton. Full details on Pedigree 8

15♀ Ann Jackson was born about 1848.

1851 Census: Aged 2, living with her parents at The Pastures, close to Primrose Hill, New ferry.

1861 Census: Aged 12, living with her parents at 6 Olinda Street, New Ferry.

21 Mar 1871: Ann married John Edwards in St Andrew's, Bebington.

15a♂ John Edwards was born about 1847 in Hawarden, Flint. John was a farmer in Frankby, also the verger in St Johns

He died in Frankby, Cheshire.

16♀ Margaret Jane Jackson was born about 1851.

1861 Census: Aged 10, living with her parents at 6 Olinda Street, New Ferry.

11 Mar 1873: Margaret married William Shackleton in St Andrew's, Bebington.

16a♂ William Shackleton was son of George Shackleton   William was born about 1848.

17♂ William Jackson was born in 1854 in New Ferry. 24 Mar 1861: He was christened in St Andrew's, Bebington.

18♀ Martha Jackson was born in 1856 in New Ferry.

6 Sep 1856: She was christened in St Andrews, Bebington.

1861 Census: Aged 5, living with her parents at 6 Olinda Street, New Ferry.

19♂ Thomas Isaac Jackson was born in Jan 1861 in 10 Grove St. New Ferry, Cheshire. Full details on Pedigree 9

20♀ Elizabeth Jackson was born in 1863 in New Ferry, Cheshire. Full details on Pedigree 9

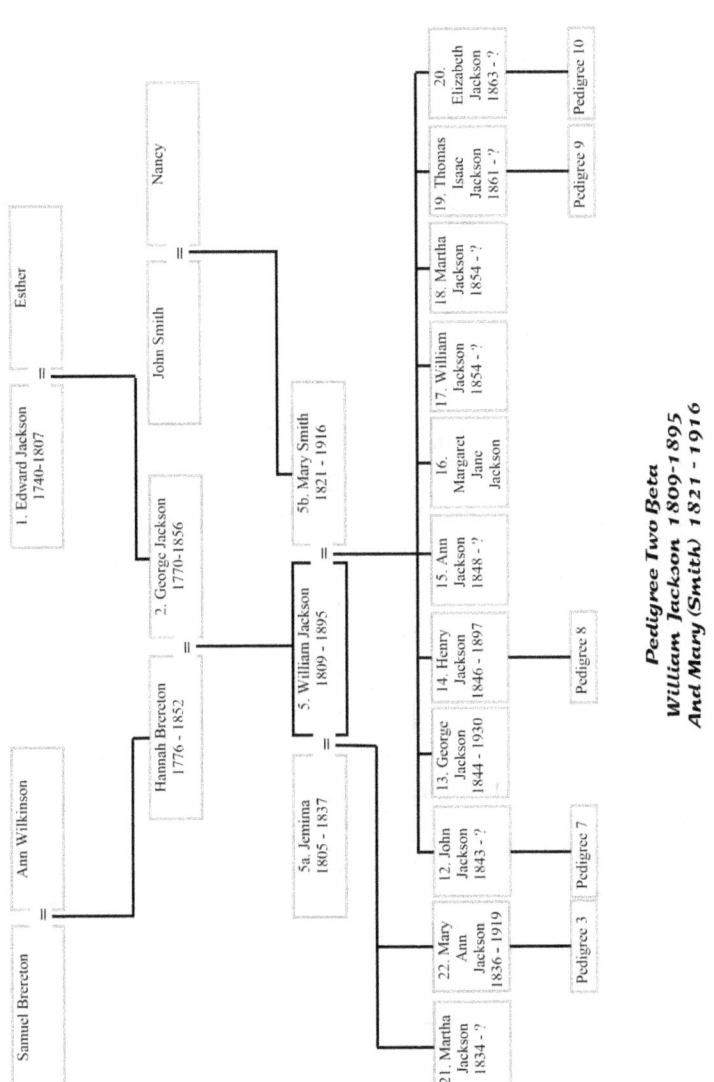

Pedigree Two Beta
William Jackson 1809-1895
And Mary (Smith) 1821 - 1916

Samuel Brereton

Ann Wilkinson

Edward Jackson
1740-1807

Esther

1. Edward Jackson
1740-1807

Hannah Brereton
1776 - 1852

2. George Jackson
1770-1856

John Smith

Nancy

5. William Jackson
1809 - 1895

5a. Jemima
1805 - 1837

5b. Mary Smith
1821 - 1916

21. Martha
Jackson
1834 - ?

22. Mary
Ann
Jackson
1836 - 1919

12. John
Jackson
1843 - ?

13. George
Jackson
1844 - 1930

14. Henry
Jackson
1846 - 1897

15. Ann
Jackson
1848 - ?

16.
Margaret
Jane
Jackson

17. William
Jackson
1854 - ?

18. Martha
Jackson
1854 - ?

19. Thomas
Isaac
Jackson
1861 - ?

20.
Elizabeth
Jackson
1863 - ?

Pedigree 3

Pedigree 7

Pedigree 8

Pedigree 9

Pedigree 10

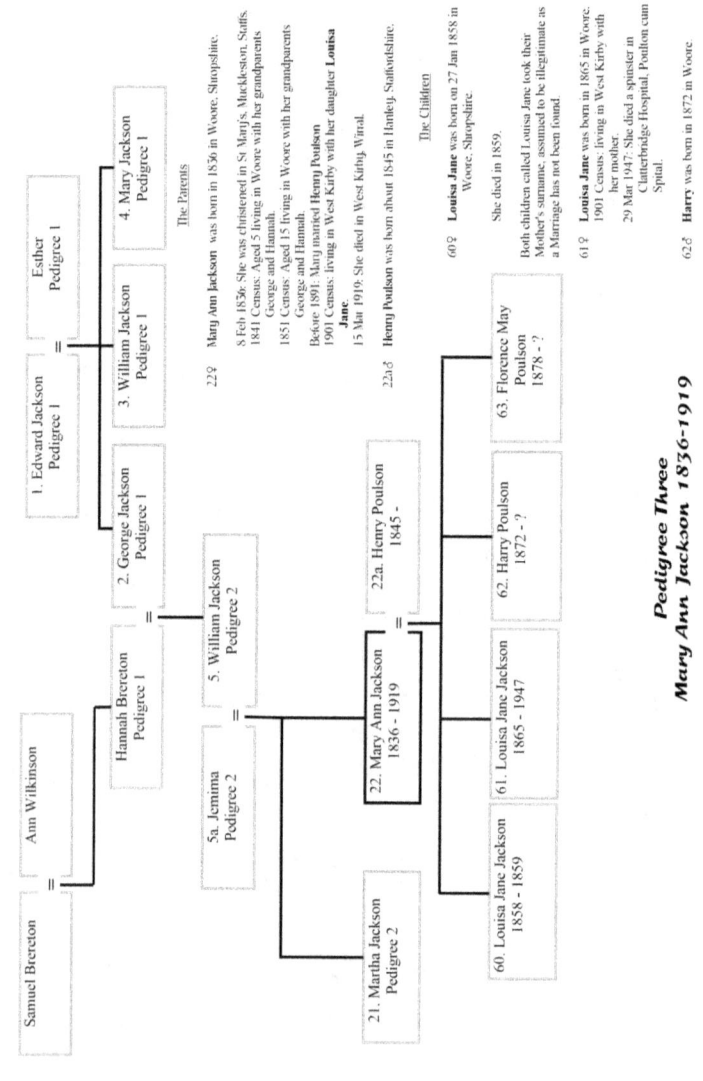

Samuel Brereton = Ann Wilkinson

1. Edward Jackson
Pedigree 1

Esther
Pedigree 1

Hannah Brereton
Pedigree 1

2. George Jackson
Pedigree 1

3. William Jackson
Pedigree 1

4. Mary Jackson
Pedigree 1

5. William Jackson
Pedigree 2

5a. Jemima
Pedigree 2

22. Mary Ann Jackson
1836 - 1919

21. Martha Jackson
Pedigree 2

23a. Henry Poulson
1845 -

60. Louisa Jane Jackson
1858 - 1859

61. Louisa Jane Jackson
1865 - 1947

62. Harry Poulson
1872 - ?

63. Florence May
Poulson
1878 - ?

The Parents

22♀ **Mary Ann Jackson** was born in 1836 in Woore, Shropshire.

8 Feb 1836: She was christened in St Mary's, Muckleston, Staffs.
1841 Census: Aged 5 living in Woore with her grandparents George and Hannah.
1851 Census: Aged 15 living in Woore with her grandparents George and Hannah.
Before 1891: Mary married **Henry Poulson**
1901 Census: living in West Kirby with her daughter **Louisa Jane**.
15 Mar 1919: She died in West Kirby Wiral.

23♂ **Henry Poulson** was born about 1845 in Hanley, Staffordshire.

The Children

60♀ **Louisa Jane** was born on 27 Jan 1858 in Woore, Shropshire.

She died in 1859.

Both children called Louisa Jane took their Mother's surname, assumed to be illegitimate as a Marriage has not been found.

61♀ **Louisa Jane** was born in 1865 in Woore.
1901 Census: living in West Kirby with her mother
29 Mar 1947: She died a spinster in Clatterbridge Hospital, Poulton cum Spital.

62♂ **Harry** was born in 1872 in Woore

63♀ **Florence May** was born in 1878.

Pedigree Three
Mary Ann Jackson 1836-1919

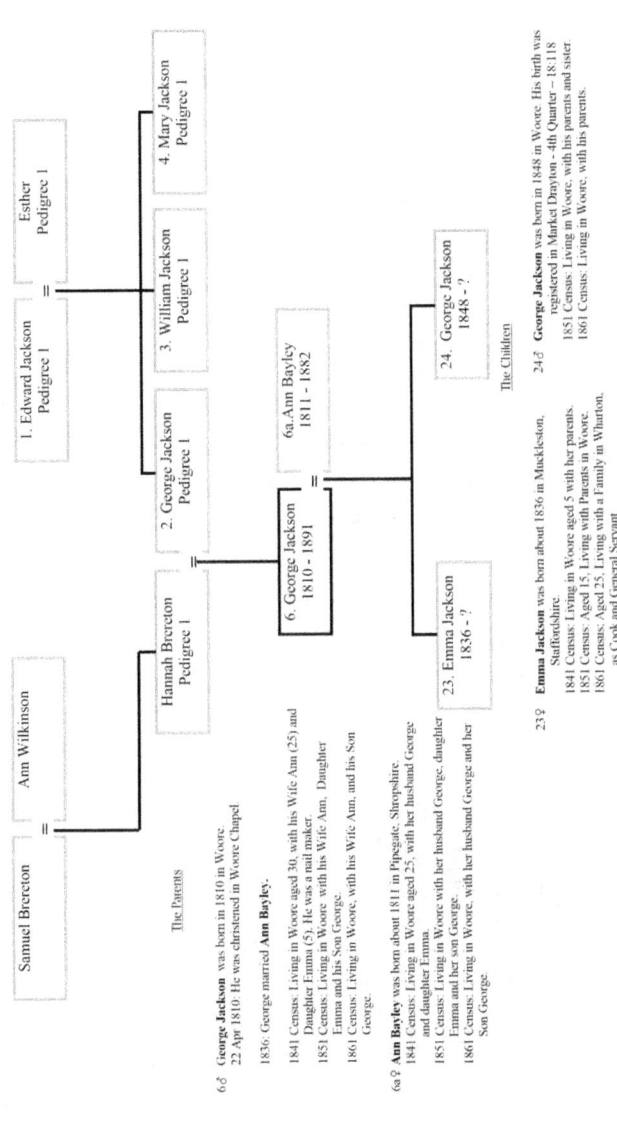

The Parents

6♂ **George Jackson** was born in 1810 in Woore.
22 Apr 1810: He was christened in Woore Chapel

1836: George married **Ann Bayley.**

1841 Census: Living in Woore aged 30, with his Wife Ann (25) and
Daughter Emma (5). He was a nail maker.
1851 Census: Living in Woore with his Wife Ann, Daughter
Emma and his Son George.
1861 Census: Living in Woore, with his Wife Ann, and his Son
George.

6a♀ **Ann Bayley** was born about 1811 in Pipegate, Shropshire.
1841 Census: Living in Woore aged 25, with her husband George
and daughter Emma.
1851 Census: Living in Woore with her husband George, daughter
Emma and her son George.
1861 Census: Living in Woore, with her husband George and her
Son George.

The Children

23♀ **Emma Jackson** was born about 1836 in Muckleston,
Staffordshire.
1841 Census: Living in Woore aged 5 with her parents.
1851 Census: Aged 15, Living with Parents in Woore.
1861 Census: Aged 25, Living with a Family in Wharton,
as Cook and General Servant

24♂ **George Jackson** was born in 1848 in Woore. His birth was
registered in Market Drayton - 4th Quarter – 18:118
1851 Census: Living in Woore, with his parents and sister
1861 Census: Living in Woore, with his parents.

Pedigree Four
George Jackson 1810 - 1891

Notes on Pedigree Five
Edward Jackson 1812 - ?

The Parents

7♂ **Edward Jackson** was born in 1812 in Woore.
16 Aug 1812: He was christened in Woore Chapel.
1842?: Edward married **Sarah Morgan.**
1851 Census: Aged 34 living in Wells street, Hanley,
Stoke upon trent, with his Wife Sarah (33) and 4
children. Martha (9) George (6) Henry (4)
Edward (2). He was an Ironmoulder.
1861 Census: Aged 48 living in 18 Elizabeth Street,
Hanley, Stoke-upon Trent, with his wife (49)
and 4 Children. George (16) A Potter, Henry
(13) a Potter. Edward (11)a Potter, Sarah (9).
1871 Census: Aged 59 living in 19 Bucknall Street,
Hanley, Stoke upon trent, with his wife (60) and
3 Children. George (25) Potter. Edward (21)
Pattern maker. Sarah (19) A Potters warehouse
woman.
1881 Census: Aged 68 living in 16 Bucknall Street,
Hanley, Stoke upon trent, with his wife (70). He
was an Iron moulder.

7a♀ **Sarah Morgan** was born about 1811 in Burslem.
Staffordshire.
1851 Census: Aged 33 living in Wells street, Hanley,
Stoke upon Trent.
1861 Census: Aged 49 living in 18 Elizabeth Street.
Hanley, Stoke-upon Trent.
1871 Census: Aged 60 living in 19 Bucknall Street.
Hanley, Stoke upon Trent.
1881 Census: Aged 70 living in 16 Bucknall Street.
Hanley, Stoke upon Trent.
1891 Census: Aged 80, a widow living at Sneyd
Green, Burslem with her Grandson (William
Simpson (Widower) aged 25 and his son,
Alfred (5)

The Children

25♀ **Martha Jackson** was born about 1842 in Hanley,
Staffordshire.
1851 Census: Aged 9 living in Wells street, Hanley,
Stoke upon trent, with her parents and siblings.

Martha married **Mr. Alcock.**

26♂ **George Jackson** was born about 1845 in Hanley.
1851 Census: Aged 6 living in Wells street, Hanley,
Stoke upon trent, with his parents and siblings.
1861 Census: Aged 16 living in 18 Elizabeth Street,
Hanley, Stoke-upon Trent, with his parents and
siblings. He was a potter.
1871 Census: Aged 25 living in 19 Bucknall Street,
Hanley, Stoke upon trent, with parents and
siblings. He was a potter.

27♂ **Henry Jackson** was born about 1847 in Hanley.
1851 Census: Aged 4 living in Wells street, Hanley,
Stoke upon trent, with his parents and siblings.
1861 Census: Aged 13 living in 18 Elizabeth Street,
Hanley, Stoke-upon Trent, with parents and
siblings. He was a potter.

28♂ **Edward Jackson** was born about 1849 in Hanley.
1851 Census: Aged 2 living in Wells street, Hanley,
Stoke upon trent, with his parents and siblings.
1861 Census: Aged 11 living in 18 Elizabeth Street,
Hanley, Stoke-upon Trent, with his his parents
and siblings. Edward was a potter.
1871 Census: Aged 21 living in 19 Bucknall Street,
Hanley, Stoke upon trent, with his parents and
siblings. He was a pattern maker.

29♀ **Sarah Jackson** was born about 1853 in Hanley.
1861 Census: Aged 9 living in 18 Elizabeth Street,
Hanley, Stoke-upon Trent, with her parents and
siblings.
1871 Census: Aged 19 living in 19 Bucknall Street.
Hanley, Stoke upon Trent, with her parents and
siblings. She was a potter's warehouse women.

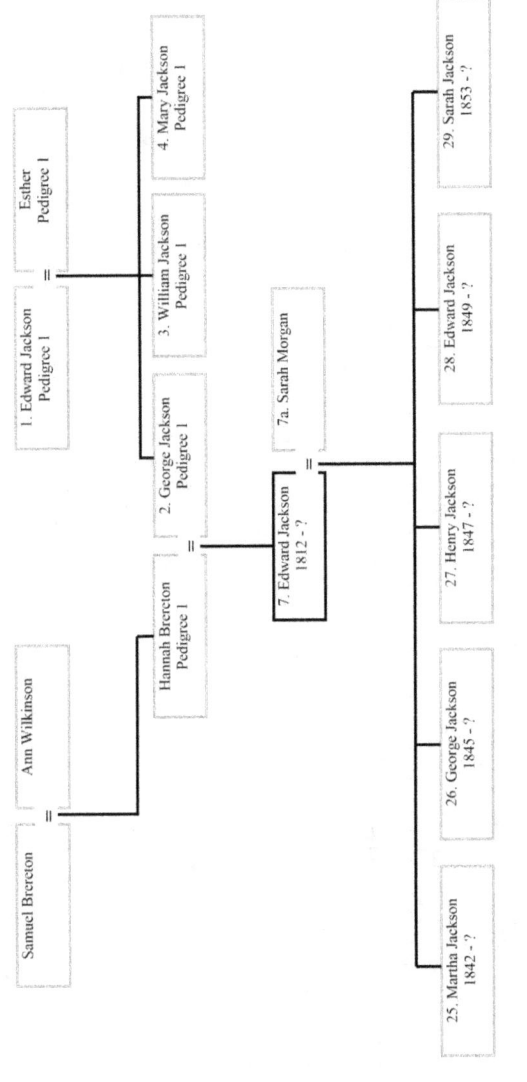

Pedigree Five
Edward Jackson 1812 - ?

Notes on Pedigree Six
Samuel Jackson 1819 - 1899

The Parents

11♂ **Samuel Jackson** was born in 1819 in Woore.
1819: Christened in Muckleston Parish Church
1840? Samuel travelled to Birkenhead with his Brother William, presumably looking for work at the newly opened Cammel Lairds Shipyards.
1841 Census: Aged 32, living in the home of Samuel Simpson and his wife Mary, in Overchurch in the Parish of Upton. Samuel was with his brother William, both Blacksmiths.

1840? Samuel married **Elizabeth Lewis.**

11a♀ **Elizabeth Lewis** daughter of William Lewis
1825? Elizabeth was born about 1825.

The Children

31♀ **Agnes Jackson** was born about 1862.

32♂ **Alan Jackson** was born in Mar 1864. His birth was registered in the 3rd Quarter in Market Drayton (ref: 6a - 715).

33♀ **Ada Jackson** was born about 1868.

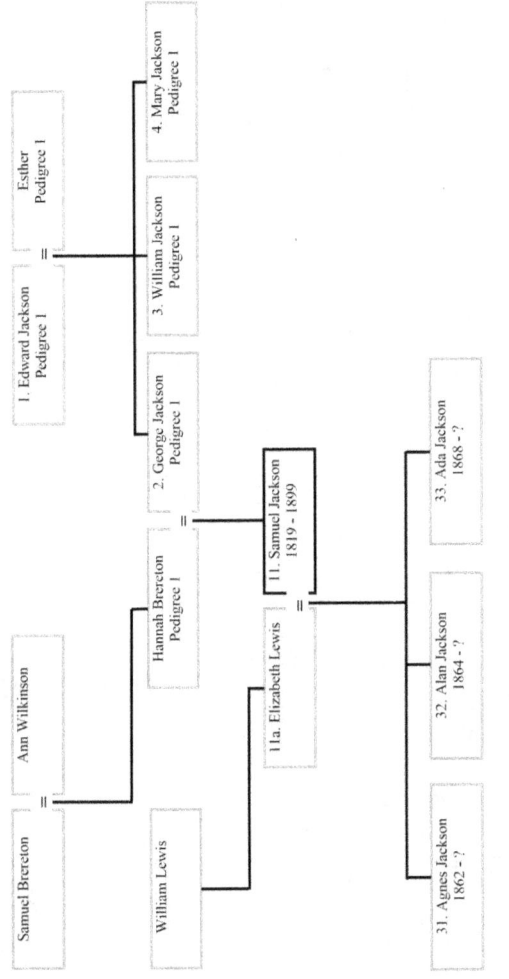

Samuel Brereton

Ann Wilkinson

=

1. Edward Jackson
Pedigree 1

Esther
Pedigree 1

=

Hannah Brereton
Pedigree 1

William Lewis

2. George Jackson
Pedigree 1

3. William Jackson
Pedigree 1

4. Mary Jackson
Pedigree 1

11. Samuel Jackson
1819 - 1899

=

11a. Elizabeth Lewis

31. Agnes Jackson
1862 - ?

32. Alan Jackson
1864 - ?

33. Ada Jackson
1868 - ?

Pedigree Six
Samuel Jackson 1819 - 1899

Notes on Pedigree Seven
John Jackson 1843 - ?

The Parents

12♂ **John Jackson** was born in 1843 in Carr, Moreton, Cheshire.
18 Jun 1843: He was christened in St. Oswald's, Bidston.
1867 approx: John married Phoebe Booth

He was buried in Bebington Cemetery.

12a♀ **Phoebe Booth** was born about 1847.

She was buried in Bebington Cemetery.

The Children

34♂ **John Smith Jackson** was born about 1868. Full details on Pedigree 11.

35♀ **Mary (Polly) Jackson** was born about 1869. Full details on Pedigree 12.

36♂ **Isaac Jackson** was born in 1873. 13 Apr 1873: He was christened.

24 Nov 1895: Isaac married **Susan O'Brian** in St. Paul's, Rock Ferry, Birkenhead.

36a♀ **Susan O'Brian** daughter of Felix O'Brian 1872: Susan was born in 54 Earl Street, Tranmere.

37♂ **George Jackson** was born in Dec 1874 in Birkenhead, Cheshire.
9 May 1875: He was christened in Birkenhead.

Dec 1901: George married **Ann Harriet Hayworth** in Birkenhead.

37a♀ **Ann Harriet Hayworth** was born about 1877.

38♀ **Louisa Jackson** was born in Sep 1877 in Birkenhead. Full details in Pedigree 13.

39♂ **William Henry Jackson** was born on 26 Sep 1879 in New Ferry Cheshire. Full details in Pedigree 14.

40♀ **Martha Jackson** was born about 1883 in New Ferry. Full details in Pedigree 15.

41♂ **Thomas Jackson** was born about 1885 in New Ferry. Full details in Pedigree 16.

42♀ **Ellen Jackson** was born about 1887 in New Ferry. Full details in Pedigree 17.

43♂ **Arthur Jackson** was born on 25 May 1890 in Grove St. New Ferry. Full details in Pedigree 18.

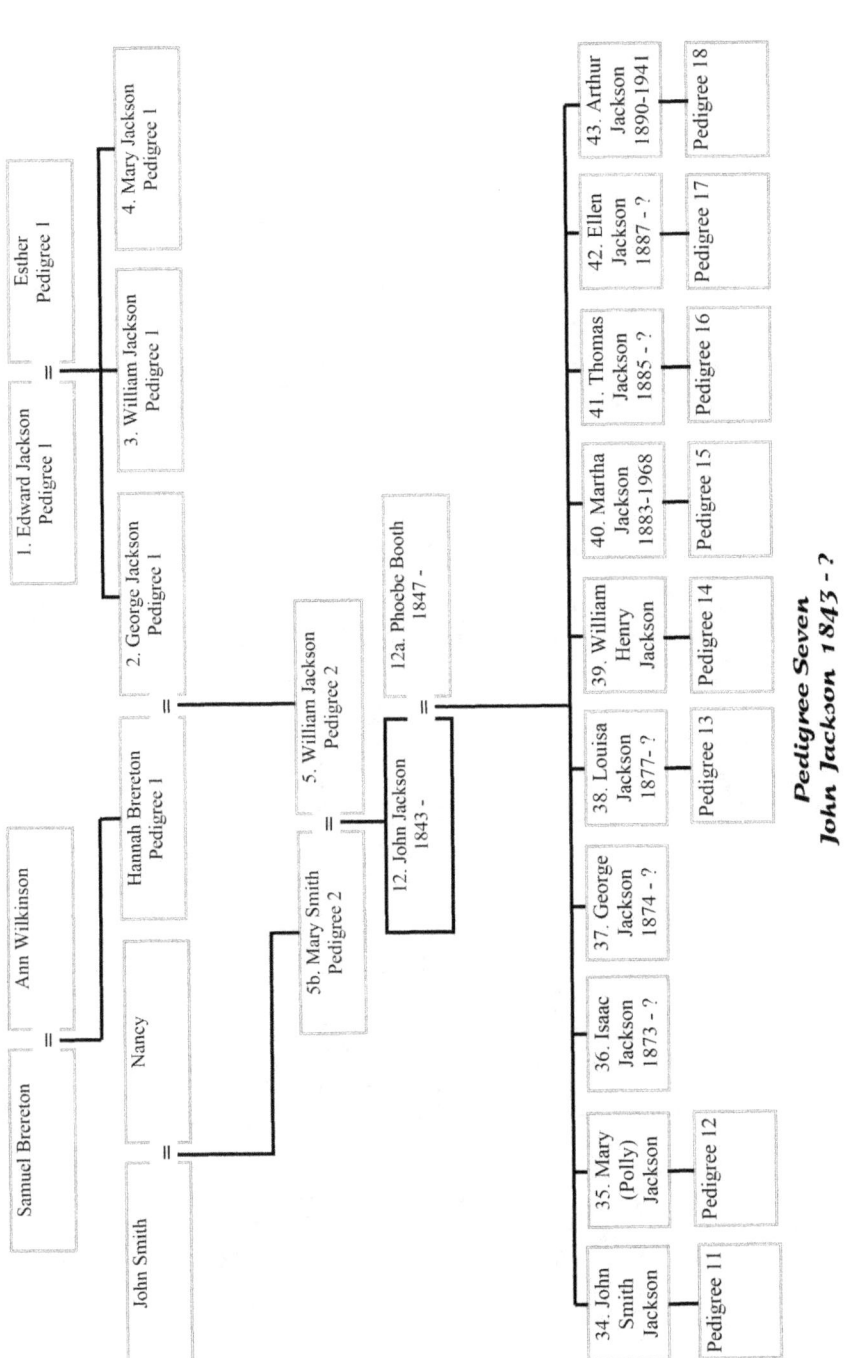

Pedigree Seven
John Jackson 1843 - ?

Pedigree Eight
Henry Jackson 1846 - 1897

The Parents

14♂ **Henry Jackson** was born on 17 Dec 1846 in Carr, Moreton.

21 Mar 1847: He was christened in St Oswald's, Bidston.

1851 Census: Aged 5, living with his parents, and Family at "Pasture"? New Ferry (in the vicinity of Primrose Hill).

1861 Census: Aged 14, living with his parents and Family, at 6 Olinda Street, New Ferry.

1871 Census: Aged 24, living with his Parents and 2 Brothers at 6 Olinda Street, New Ferry.

24 Dec 1874: Henry married **Fanny Griffiths** in St Andrew's Church, Bebington.

1881 Census: Aged 34, living with his Wife and Family at 6 Manley Place, New Ferry.

1891 Census: Aged 44, living with his Wife and Family at 19 Brunswick Street, Tranmere Lillian 14, Harry 13, Annie 11, Louisa 10.

9 Jan 1897: He died aged 51 in Tranmere Workhouse.

12 Jan 1897: He was buried in Bebington Cemetery (Common Grave).

14a♀ **Fanny Griffiths** daughter of James Griffiths and Caroline Davies.

9 Apr 1850: Fanny was born in Phoebe's Court, Blake Street, Liverpool. The courts were notoriously poor accommodation with no sanitary conditions and no running water.

1851 Census: Aged 11 months, living with her parents and three older children at 2, Phebe Place, Blake Street, Liverpool.

1861 Census: Aged 10. Living with her parents and four other children at 6, Derby Place, Liverpool.

1871 Census: Aged 20, No trace.

24 Dec 1874 married Henry.

1881 Census: Aged 30, Living with her Husband and Children at 6 Manley place, Lower Bebington.

9 Jan 1897 Henry died.

1901 Census: Living with Lilian and her husband, Joseph Parsons at 126 New Chester Road with her two other daughters Annie and Louisa.

30 Nov 1909. She died in 2 Clare St, Lower Tranmere, Cheshire.

The Children

44♀ **Lilian Alice Jackson** was born in Apr 1876 in New Ferry. Full details in Pedigree 19.

45♂ **Harry Jackson** was born on 10 Mar 1878 in 6 Manley Place, New Ferry. Full details in Pedigree 20.

46♀ **Annie Jackson** was born on 21 Feb 1880 in Birkenhead, Cheshire.

1891 Census: Aged 11. Living with her parents at 19 Brunswick Street, Tranmere.

1901 Census: Living with her parents at 126 New Chester Road.

Dec 1901: Annie married **Thomas Burrows** in Birkenhead.

46a♂ **Thomas Burrows** was born about 1880.

47♀ **Louisa Jackson** was born in the third quarter of 1881 (ref: 8a 441) in Birkenhead. Full details in Pedigree 21

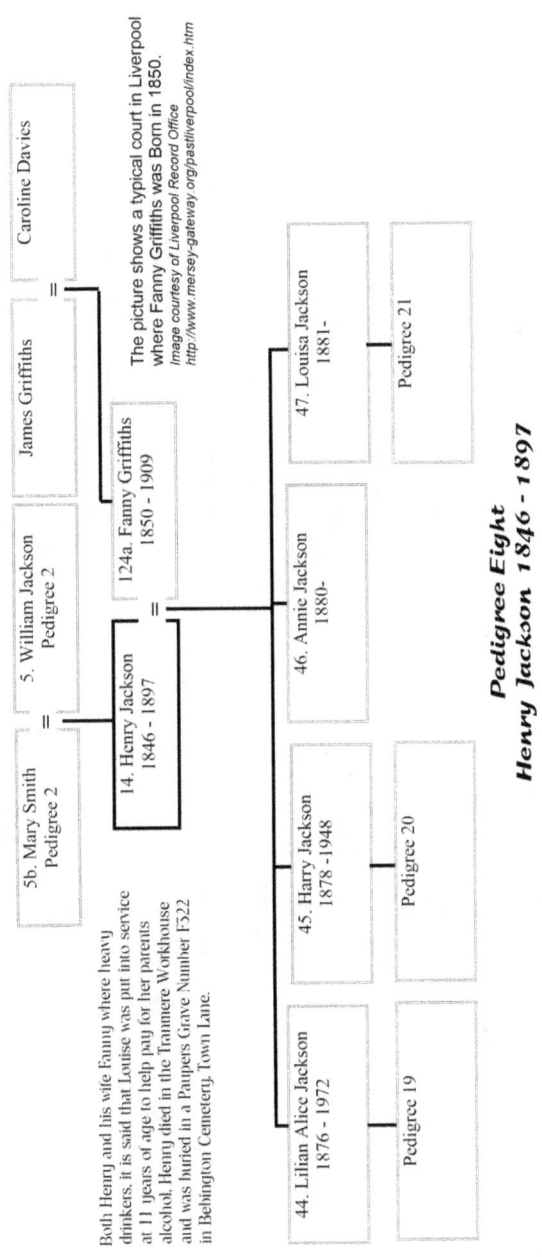

Caroline Davies

James Griffiths

= =

The picture shows a typical court in Liverpool where Fanny Griffiths was Born in 1850.
Image courtesy of Liverpool Record Office
http://www.mersey-gateway.org/pastliverpool/index.htm

5. William Jackson
Pedigree 2

124a. Fanny Griffiths
1850 - 1909

5b. Mary Smith
Pedigree 2

= =

14. Henry Jackson
1846 - 1897

=

Both Henry and his wife Fanny where heavy drinkers, it is said that Louise was put into service at 11 years of age to help pay for her parents alcohol. Henry died in the Tranmere Workhouse and was buried in a Paupers Grave Number F522 in Bebington Cemetery, Town Lane.

47. Louisa Jackson
1881-

46. Annie Jackson
1880-

45. Harry Jackson
1878 -1948

44. Lilian Alice Jackson
1876 - 1972

Pedigree 21

Pedigree 20

Pedigree 19

Pedigree Eight
Henry Jackson 1846 - 1897

Notes on Pedigree Nine
Thomas Isaac Jackson 1861 - ?

The Parents

19♂ **Thomas Isaac Jackson** was born in Jan 1861 at 10 Grove St. New Ferry, Cheshire. [ref: 1st Quarter, Wirral, Cheshire, 8a 570]

24 Mar 1861: He was christened in St. Andrew's, Bebington.

1861 Census: Aged 3 months, living with his parents at 6 Olinda Street, New Ferry.

13 Jul 1885: Thomas married **Jane Formby** in St. Paul's Presbyterian Church, Church Road, Tranmere, Birkenhead.

1888 - 1897 fathered five children by Jane.

1900: Jane died.

Later Thomas married Kathleen but had no children by the marriage.

During his life, Thomas Isaac worked at Cammel Lairds as a Joiner and later had a chip shop at 11, Crofton Road Lower Tranmere.

19a♀ **Jane Formby** daughter of James (John) Formby Jane was born in Hightown, (Huyton)? Lancs. [2nd Qtr 1860, West Derby 6b - 361]

1871 Census: Living with her Parents aged 10.

1885 married Thomas.

1888 - 1897 gave birth to five children.

1900: She died in in Birkenhead.

The Children

48♂ **Harold Jackson** was born about 1888.

49♀ **Edith Fanny Jackson** was born about 1889 in Birkenhead.
She died in 1896 in Birkenhead. aged 7 [Death Cert - 3rd Qrtr 1896 Birkenhead 8a - 308]

50♂ **William Jackson** was born in 1891.
23 Apr 1891: He was christened in St. Paul's, Rock Ferry.

51♂. **Charles Jackson** was born about 1892.

52♂ **Frank Jackson** was born about 1897 in Birkenhead.
1924: Frank married **Lavinia Whittington** in Birkenhead.

52a♀ **Lavinia Whittington** was born about 1903 in Birkenhead.

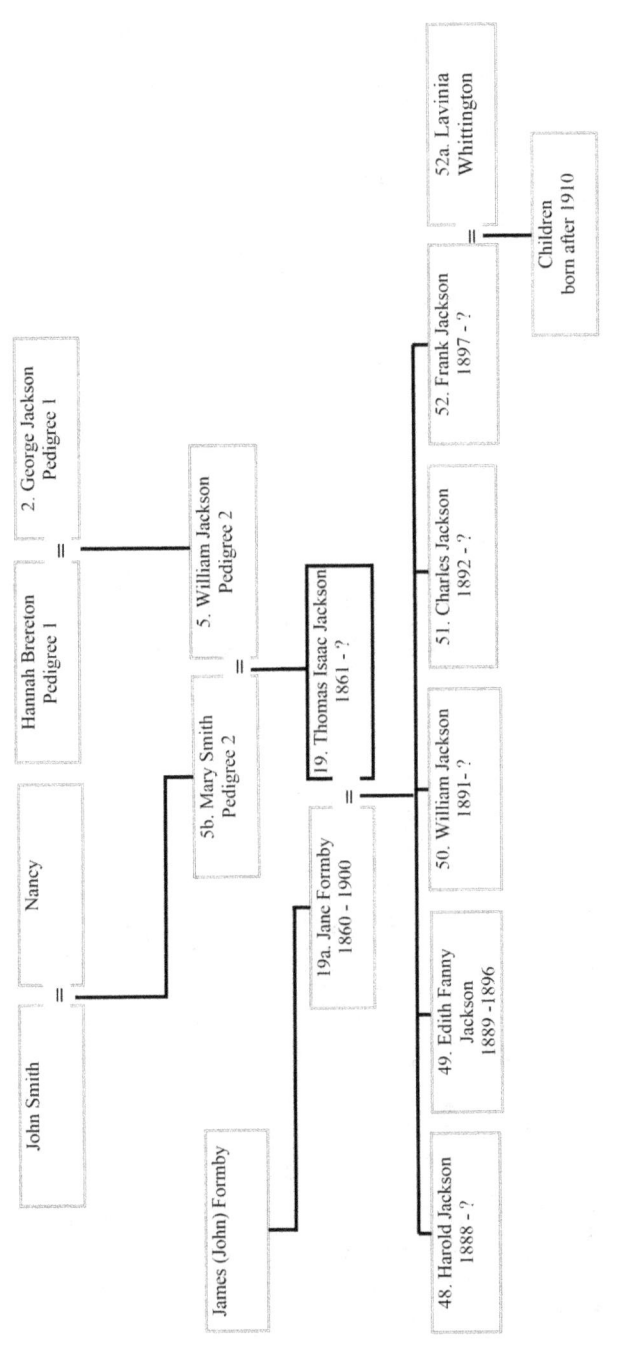

John Smith == Nancy

Hannah Brereton
Pedigree 1

==

2. George Jackson
Pedigree 1

5b. Mary Smith
Pedigree 2

5. William Jackson
Pedigree 2

==

James (John) Formby

19a. Jane Formby
1860 - 1900

==

19. Thomas Isaac Jackson
1861 - ?

48. Harold Jackson
1888 - ?

49. Edith Fanny
Jackson
1889 -1896

50. William Jackson
1891 - ?

51. Charles Jackson
1892 - ?

52. Frank Jackson
1897 - ?

==

52a. Lavinia
Whittington

Children
born after 1910

Pedigree Nine
Thomas Isaac Jackson 1861 - ?

The Parents

20% Elizabeth Jackson was born in 1863 in New Ferry, Cheshire. 30 Aug 1863: She was christened in St. Andrew's, Bebington. 1871 Census: Aged 7 living with her parents and siblings at 6 Olinda Street, New Ferry. 24 Sep 1887: Elizabeth married Henry Edward Phillips in St Marys, Edgehill, Liverpool.

20a% Henry Edward Phillips was born about 1863 in Garston, Liverpool. 1917: He died and was buried in Bebington Cemetery, Town Lane, Bebington.

The Children

55% Frederick Phillips was born about 1889. He died an infant.

54% Herbert Henry Phillips was born about 1891. 1920: Herbert married Jean O'Hanlon. Worked at Levers Glycerine Refinery. He was buried in Landican Crematorium, Arrowe Park.

54a% Jean O'Hanlon born about 1895 in Georgetown, Dumfries. She died in Clatterbridge Hospital.

55% Gertrude Phillips was born about 1893. 1914: Gertrude married Percival Day. The marriage ended in divorce. She was buried in Bebington Cemetery, Town Lane, Bebington.

55a% Percival Day was born about 1890.

56% Frank Edward Phillips was born about 1895 in 37 Wycliff St. Rock Ferry. During the First World War he was in the Cheshire Regiment and survived a gassing at The Somme. Frank married Doris Whittle. During the Second World War he was a Captain in Royal Ordnance Corps. Frank and Doris' children were born after 1910.

58% Catherine Elizabeth Jones was the daughter of Berwyn Jones and Elizabeth Hughes. 30 Oct 1898: She was born in Cardigan Street, Birkenhead.1 15 Aug 1974: She died and was buried in Landican Crematorium, Arrowe Park.

58% George Frederick Phillips was born on 15 Nov 1900 at 35 Wycliff St. Rock Ferry. 24 Jun 1925: George married Catherine Elizabeth Jones in St James's, Birkenhead.

50% Dora Lilian Phillips was born about 1903 in 55 Wycliff St. Rock Ferry. 1927: Dora married Harold Fenner in St Andrews, Bebington. Their daughter, Doreen, was born after 1910. 1987: Dora Lilian died in Australia.

50a% Harold Fenner died about 1987 in Australia.

57% Winifred Ada Phillips was born about 1898 in 55 Wycliff St. Rock Ferry. 1920: Winifred married Joseph Bartley in St Paul's, Rock Ferry.

57a% Joseph Bartley was born about 1896. 1965?: He died about 1965.

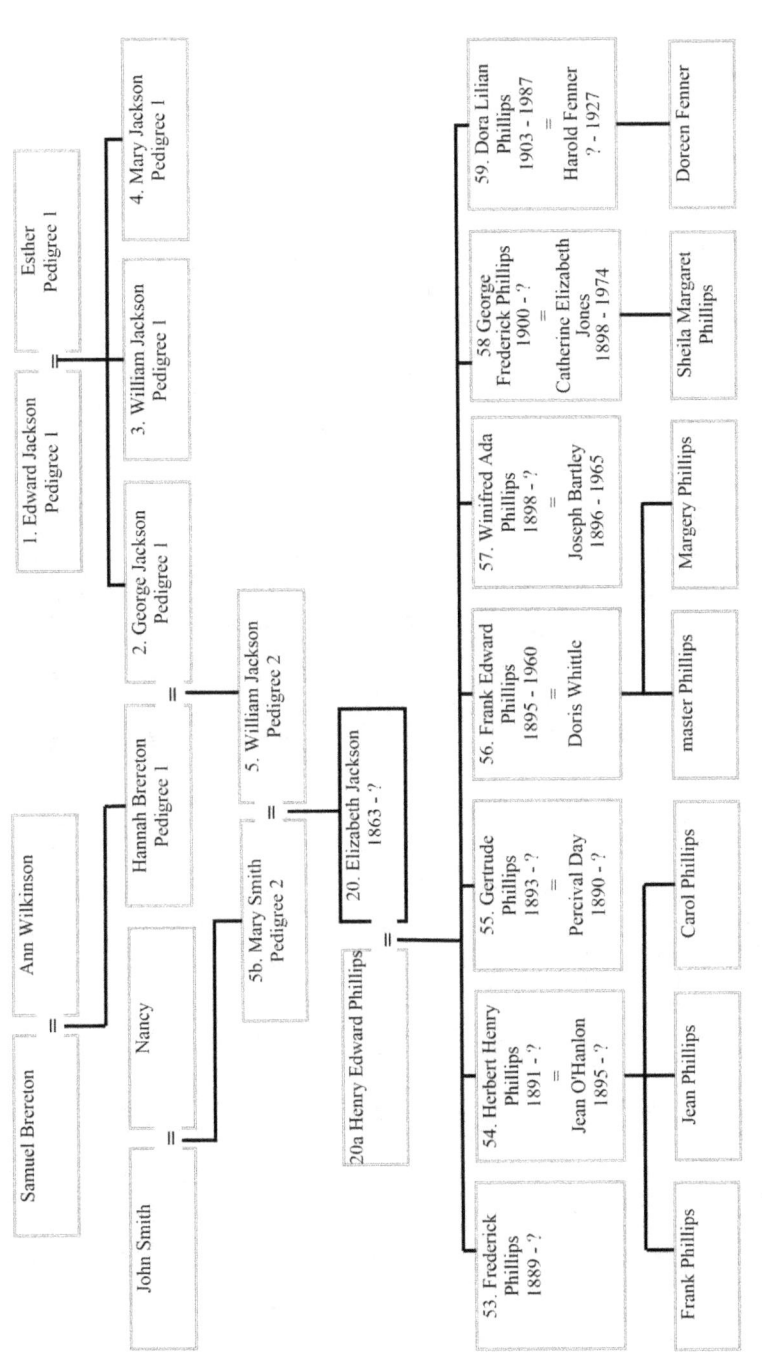

Pedigree Ten
Elizabeth Jackson 1863 - ?

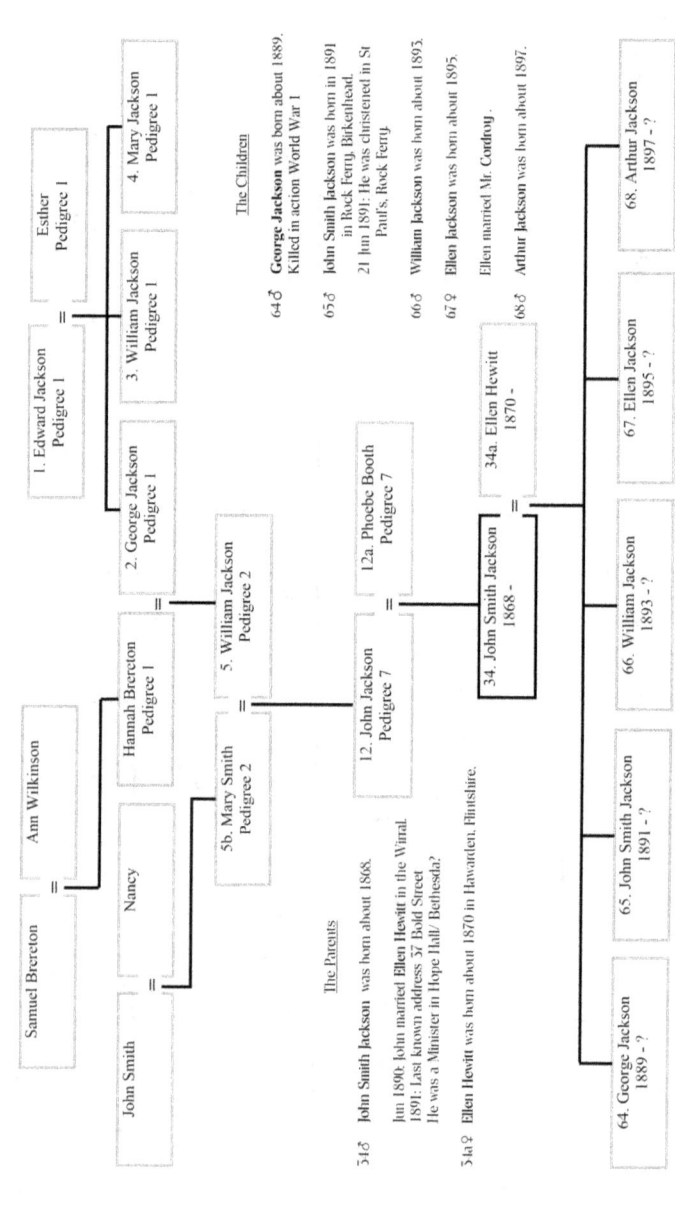

Samuel Brereton

Ann Wilkinson

John Smith

Nancy

John Smith

=

Hannah Brereton
Pedigree 1

=

1. Edward Jackson
Pedigree 1

=

Esther
Pedigree 1

2. George Jackson
Pedigree 1

3. William Jackson
Pedigree 1

4. Mary Jackson
Pedigree 1

5b. Mary Smith
Pedigree 2

=

5. William Jackson
Pedigree 2

12. John Jackson
Pedigree 7

=

12a. Phoebe Booth
Pedigree 7

34. John Smith Jackson
1868 -

=

34a. Ellen Hewitt
1870 -

64. George Jackson
1889 - ?

65. John Smith Jackson
1891 - ?

66. William Jackson
1893 - ?

67. Ellen Jackson
1895 - ?

68. Arthur Jackson
1897 - ?

The Parents

5 1 ♂   **John Smith Jackson** was born about 1868.

Jun 1890: John married **Ellen Hewitt** in the Wirral.
1891: Last known address 57 Bold Street
He was a Minister in Hope Hall/ Bethesda?

5 1a ♀   **Ellen Hewitt** was born about 1870 in Hawarden, Flintshire.

The Children

64 ♂   **George Jackson** was born about 1889.
Killed in action World War 1

65 ♂   **John Smith Jackson** was born in 1891 in Rock Ferry, Birkenhead.
21 Jun 1891: He was christened in St Paul's, Rock Ferry.

66 ♂   **William Jackson** was born about 1893.

67 ♀   **Ellen Jackson** was born about 1895.
Ellen married Mr. Cordroy.

68 ♂   **Arthur Jackson** was born about 1897.

Pedigree Eleven
John Smith Jackson 1868 - ?

Morton Brickworks circa 1900
Harry Jackson extreme left.
See Pedigree 20

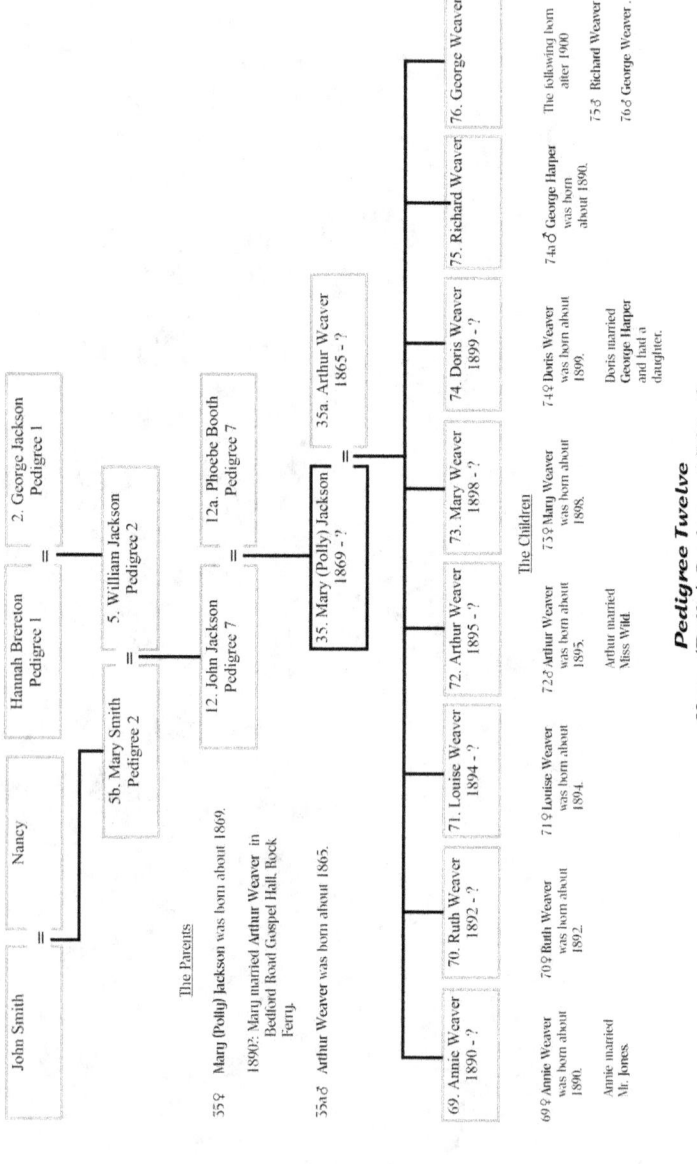

John Smith ═ Nancy

Hannah Brereton
Pedigree 1
═
2. George Jackson
Pedigree 1

5b. Mary Smith
Pedigree 2
═
5. William Jackson
Pedigree 2

12. John Jackson
Pedigree 7
═
12a. Phoebe Booth
Pedigree 7

The Parents

35. Mary (Polly) Jackson
1869 - ?
═
35a. Arthur Weaver
1865 - ?

35♀ **Mary (Polly) Jackson** was born about 1869.

1890?. Mary married **Arthur Weaver** in Bedford Road Gospel Hall, Rock Ferry.

35a♂ **Arthur Weaver** was born about 1865.

69. Annie Weaver
1890 - ?

70. Ruth Weaver
1892 - ?

71. Louise Weaver
1894 - ?

72. Arthur Weaver
1895 - ?

73. Mary Weaver
1898 - ?

74. Doris Weaver
1899 - ?

75. Richard Weaver

76. George Weaver

The Children

69♀ **Annie Weaver** was born about 1890.

Annie married Mr. Jones.

70♀ **Ruth Weaver** was born about 1892.

71♀ **Louise Weaver** was born about 1894.

72♂ **Arthur Weaver** was born about 1895.

Arthur married Miss Wild.

73♀ **Mary Weaver** was born about 1898.

74♀ **Doris Weaver** was born about 1899.

Doris married **George Harper** and had a daughter.

74a♂ **George Harper** was born about 1890.

The following born after 1900

75♂ **Richard Weaver**

76♂ **George Weaver** .

Pedigree Twelve
Mary (Polly) Jackson 1869 - ?

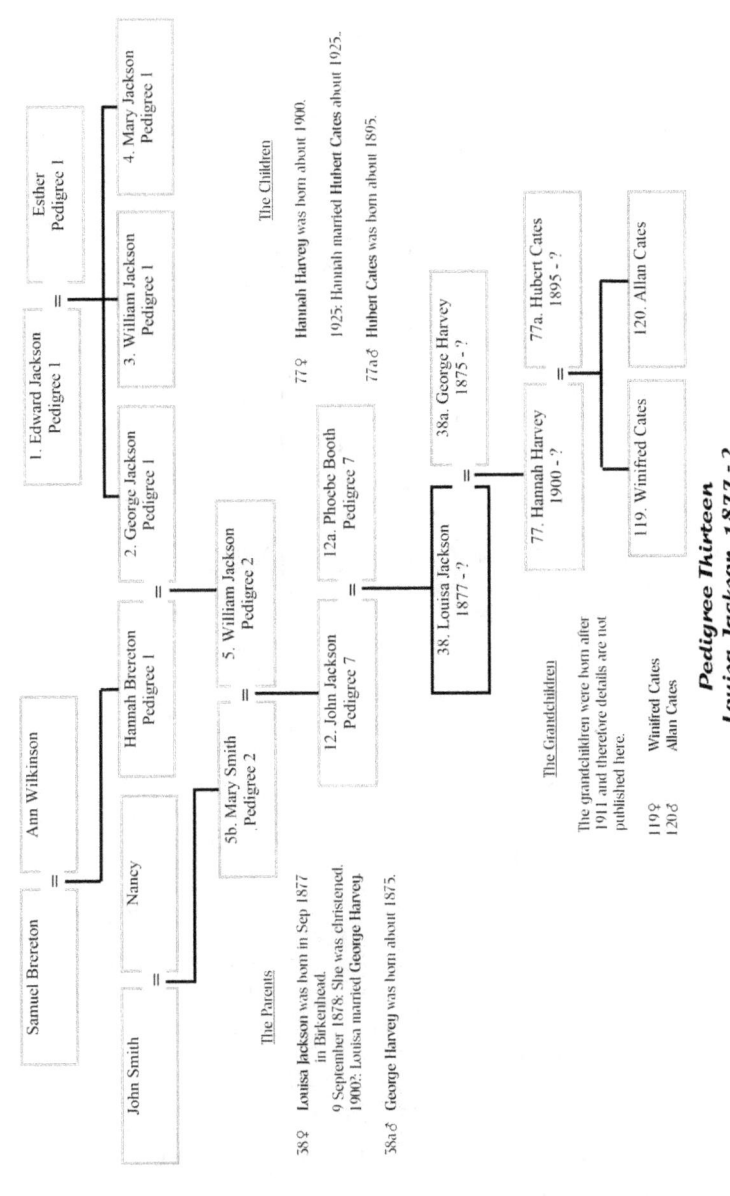

Samuel Brereton = Ann Wilkinson

Edward Jackson
Pedigree 1
=
Esther
Pedigree 1

1. Edward Jackson
Pedigree 1

2. George Jackson
Pedigree 1

3. William Jackson
Pedigree 1

4. Mary Jackson
Pedigree 1

John Smith
=
Nancy

Hannah Brereton
Pedigree 1
=
5. William Jackson
Pedigree 2

5b. Mary Smith
Pedigree 2
=
12. John Jackson
Pedigree 7

12a. Phoebe Booth
Pedigree 7

38. Louisa Jackson
1877 - ?
=
38a. George Harvey
1875 - ?

77. Hannah Harvey
1900 - ?
=
77a. Hubert Cates
1895 - ?

119. Winifred Cates

120. Allan Cates

The Parents

38♀ **Louisa Jackson** was born in Sep 1877 in Birkenhead.
9 September 1878: She was christened.
1900: Louisa married **George Harvey.**

38a♂ **George Harvey** was born about 1875.

The Children

77♀ **Hannah Harvey** was born about 1900.
1925: Hannah married **Hubert Cates** about 1925.

77a♂ **Hubert Cates** was born about 1895.

The Grandchildren

The grandchildren were born after 1911 and therefore details are not published here.

119♀ Winifred Cates
120♂ Allan Cates

Pedigree Thirteen
Louisa Jackson 1877 - ?

The Parents

39♂ **William Henry Jackson** was born on
26 Sep 1879 in New Ferry Cheshire.
19 Sep 1910: William married **Laura
Millington McArdle** in St Bedes.
Toxteth, Liverpool.
14 Nov 1937: He died at 98
Woodward Rd. Rock Ferry.
18 Nov 1937: He was buried in
Bebington Cemetery.
He was a woodcase maker for Lever
Bros, Port Sunlight

39♀ **Laura Millington McArdle** daughter
of Henry McArdle and Martha
Stevenson.
1 Oct 1881: Laura was born at 242
Old Chester Road, Rock Ferry.
19 Sep 1910: married **William**.
19 Apr 1965: She died in 147 Prenton
Hall Road, Prenton,
Birkenhead.
24 Apr 1965: She was buried in
Bebington Cemetery.

The Children
The children were born after 1911 and
therefore details are not published here.

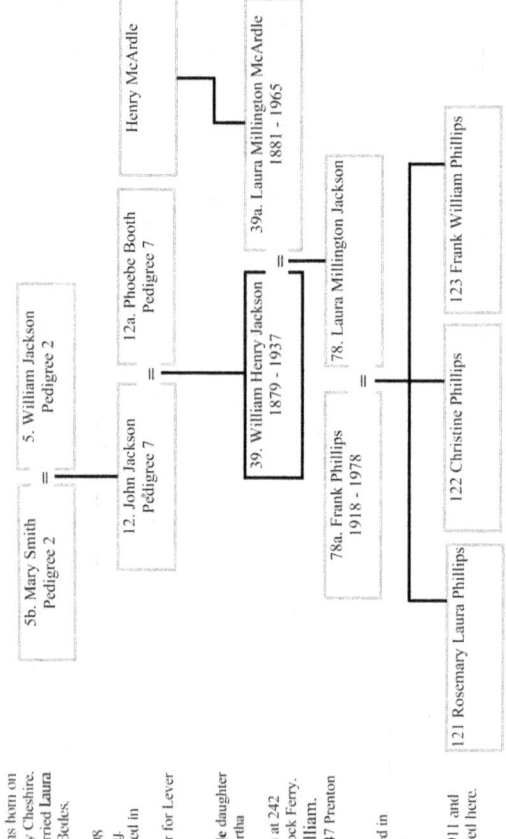

Henry McArdle

5. William Jackson
Pedigree 2

5b. Mary Smith
Pedigree 2

12a. Phoebe Booth
Pedigree 7

39a. Laura Millington McArdle
1881 - 1965

12. John Jackson
Pedigree 7

39. William Henry Jackson
1879 - 1937

78a. Frank Phillips
1918 - 1978

78. Laura Millington Jackson

123 Frank William Phillips

122 Christine Phillips

121 Rosemary Laura Phillips

Pedigree Fourteen
William Henry Jackson 1879 - 1937

The Armchair, Moreton *circa* 1906.
A Hawthorne hedge, shaped into an armchair by the Farmer George Smith,
seated in the chair is Sarah Lilian Jackson, with her mother Martha Ellen to her left (in the dark dress)
A Pub called the Armchair now stands near to this spot.
See Pedigree 20

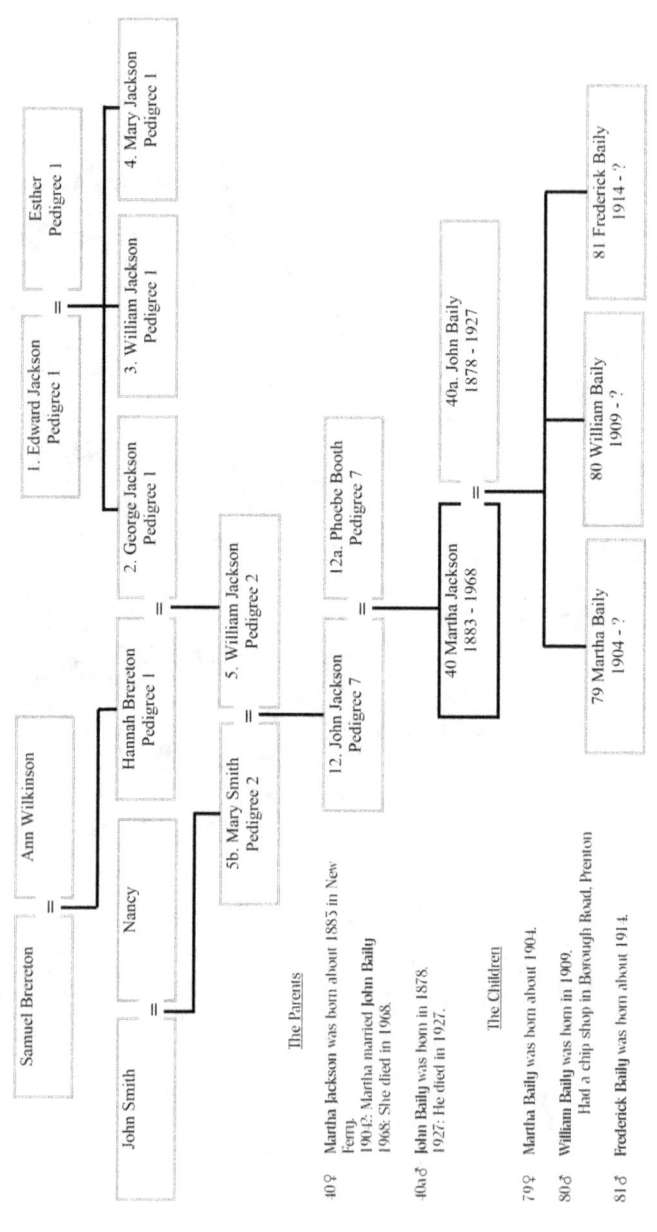

	Samuel Brereton	=	Ann Wilkinson					Edward Jackson Pedigree 1	=	Esther Pedigree 1	

John Smith

Nancy

Hannah Brereton
Pedigree 1

2. George Jackson
Pedigree 1

3. William Jackson
Pedigree 1

4. Mary Jackson
Pedigree 1

1. Edward Jackson
Pedigree 1

=

5b. Mary Smith
Pedigree 2

5. William Jackson
Pedigree 2

12. John Jackson
Pedigree 7

12a. Phoebe Booth
Pedigree 7

40 Martha Jackson
1883 - 1968

40a. John Baily
1878 - 1927

79 Martha Baily
1904 - ?

80 William Baily
1909 - ?

81 Frederick Baily
1914 - ?

The Parents

40♀ **Martha Jackson** was born about 1883 in New Ferry.
1904: Martha married **John Baily**
1968: She died in 1968.

40a♂ **John Baily** was born in 1878.
1927: He died in 1927.

The Children

79♀ **Martha Baily** was born about 1904.

80♂ **William Baily** was born in 1909.
Had a chip shop in Borough Road, Prenton

81♂ **Frederick Baily** was born about 1914.

Pedigree Fifteen
Martha Jackson 1883 - 1968

Harry Jackson and Family
Digg Lane, Moreton *circa* 1908
See Pedigree 20:

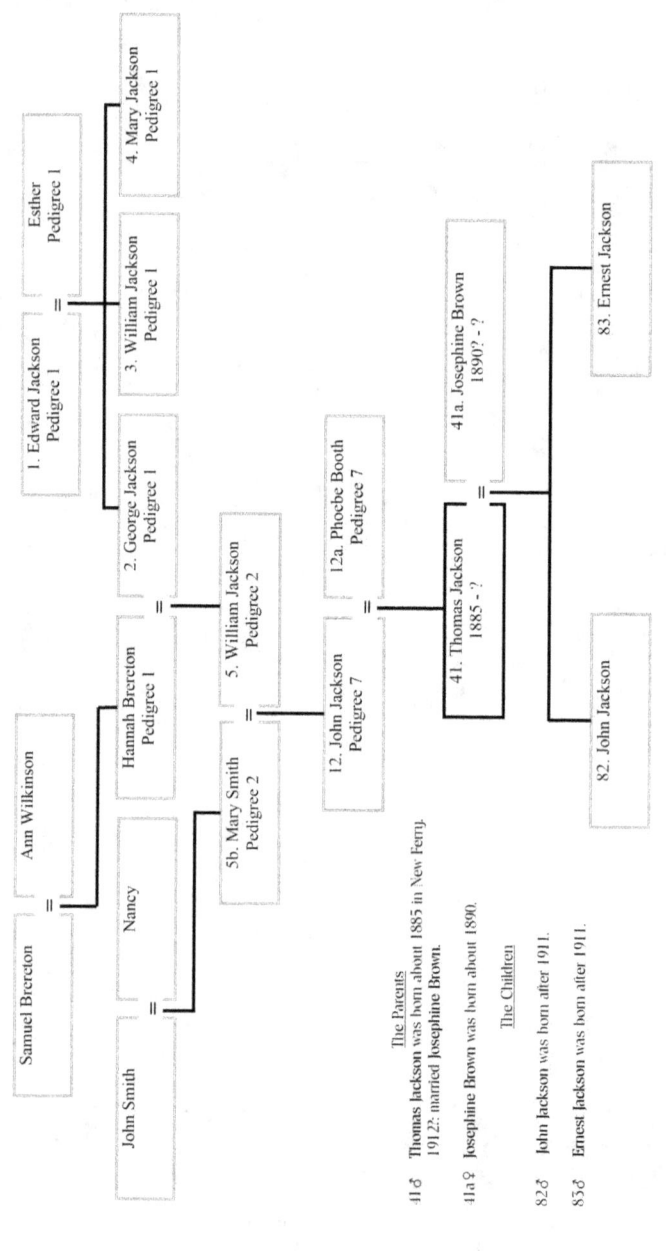

Samuel Brereton = Ann Wilkinson

John Smith = Nancy

1. Edward Jackson
Pedigree 1

=

Esther
Pedigree 1

2. George Jackson
Pedigree 1

3. William Jackson
Pedigree 1

4. Mary Jackson
Pedigree 1

Hannah Brereton
Pedigree 1

=

5. William Jackson
Pedigree 2

5b. Mary Smith
Pedigree 2

=

12. John Jackson
Pedigree 7

12a. Phoebe Booth
Pedigree 7

=

41. Thomas Jackson
1885 - ?

41a. Josephine Brown
1890? - ?

=

82. John Jackson

83. Ernest Jackson

The Parents

41 ♂ **Thomas Jackson** was born about 1885 in New Ferry.
1912: married Josephine Brown.

41a ♀ **Josephine Brown** was born about 1890.

The Children

82 ♂ **John Jackson** was born after 1911.

85 ♂ **Ernest Jackson** was born after 1911.

Pedigree Sixteen
Thomas Jackson 1885 - ?

Nellie Jackson : Charles Henry Jackson : Sarah Lilian Jackson ; *circa* 1920
See pedigree 20

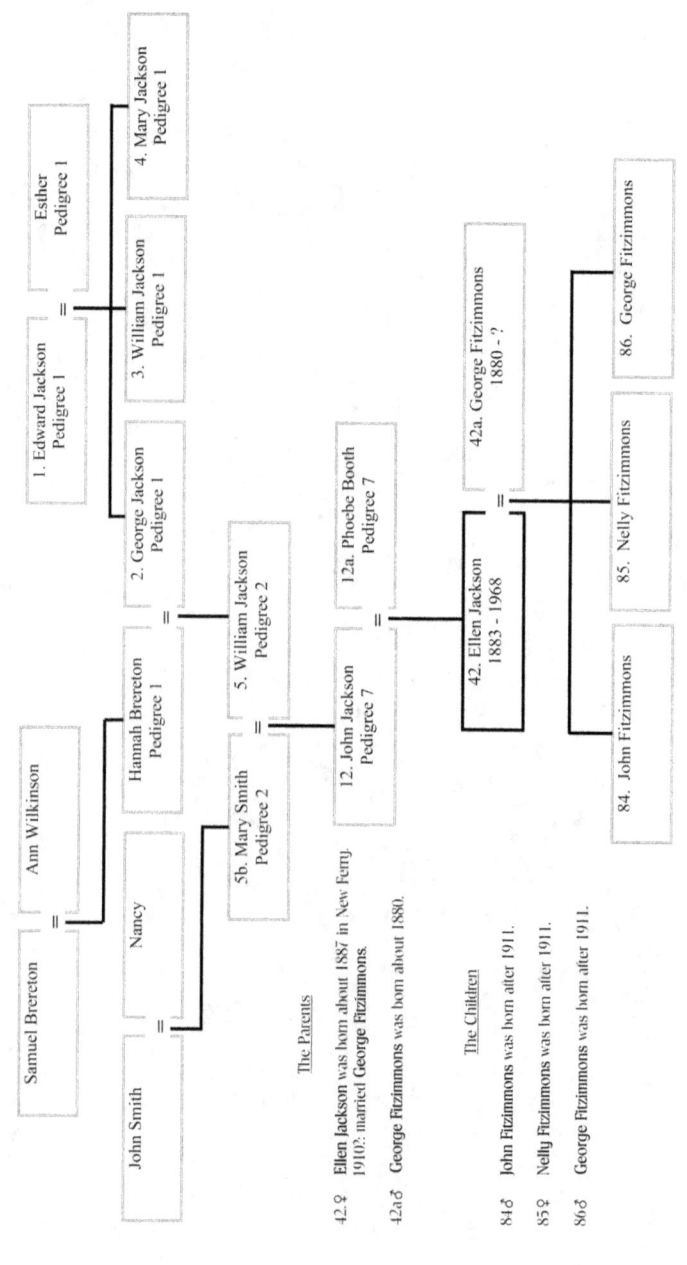

The Parents

42.♀ **Ellen Jackson** was born about 1887 in New Ferry. 1910?. married **George Fitzimmons**.

42a♂ **George Fitzimmons** was born about 1880.

The Children

84♂ **John Fitzimmons** was born after 1911.

85♀ **Nelly Fitzimmons** was born after 1911.

86♂ **George Fitzimmons** was born after 1911.

Pedigree Seventeen
Ellen Jackson 1887 -

Harry and Martha Jackson *circa* 1928 at 1, Agnes Road, Tranmere
See Pedigree 20

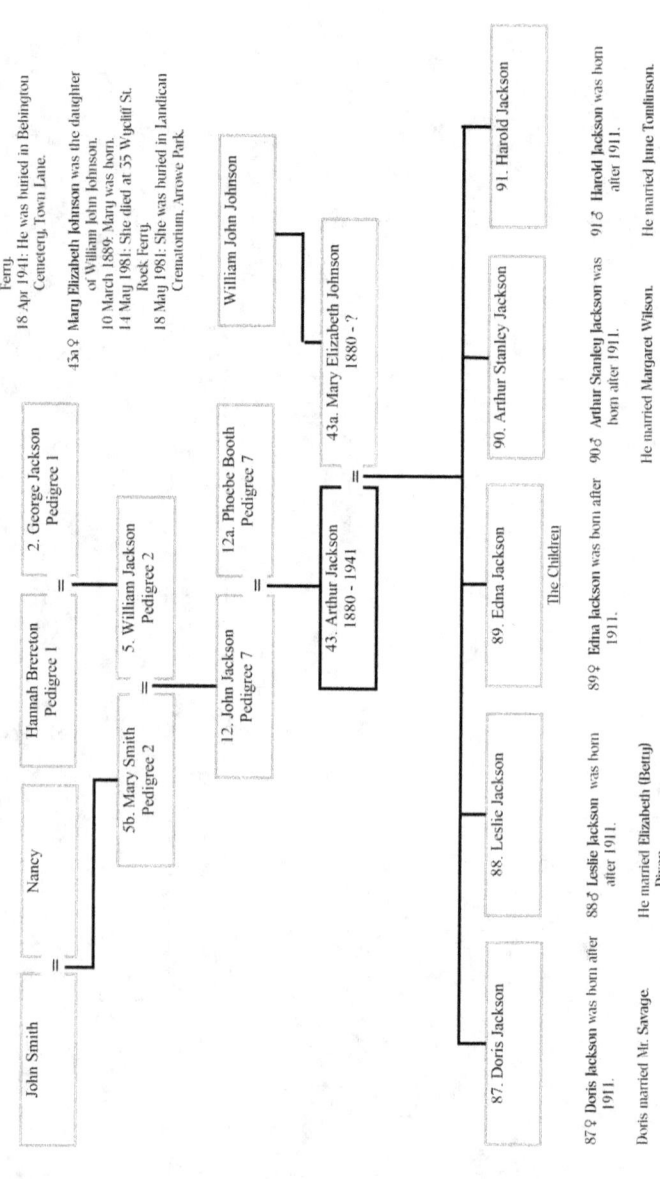

The Parents

45♂ **Arthur Jackson** was born on 25 May 1890 in Grove St. New Ferry.
29 Dec 1913: Arthur married **Mary Elizabeth Johnson**.
14 Apr 1941: He died at 55 Wycliff St. Rock Ferry.
18 Apr 1941: He was buried in Bebington Cemetery, Town Lane.

45♀ **Mary Elizabeth Johnson** was the daughter of William John Johnson.
10 March 1889: Mary was born.
14 May 1981: She died at 55 Wycliff St. Rock Ferry.
18 May 1981: She was buried in Landican Crematorium, Arrowe Park.

Boxes:

John Smith = Nancy

Hannah Brereton Pedigree 1 = 2. George Jackson Pedigree 1

5b. Mary Smith Pedigree 2 = 5. William Jackson Pedigree 2

12. John Jackson Pedigree 7 = 12a. Phoebe Booth Pedigree 7

William John Johnson

43. Arthur Jackson 1880 - 1941 = 43a. Mary Elizabeth Johnson 1880 - ?

The Children

87. Doris Jackson
88. Leslie Jackson
89. Edna Jackson
90. Arthur Stanley Jackson
91. Harold Jackson

87♀ **Doris Jackson** was born after 1911.
Doris married Mr. Savage.

88♂ **Leslie Jackson** was born after 1911.
He married Elizabeth (Betty) Dixon.

89♀ **Edna Jackson** was born after 1911.

90♂ **Arthur Stanley Jackson** was born after 1911.
He married Margaret Wilson.

91♂ **Harold Jackson** was born after 1911.
He married June Tomlinson.

Pedigree Eighteen
Arthur Jackson 1880 - 1941

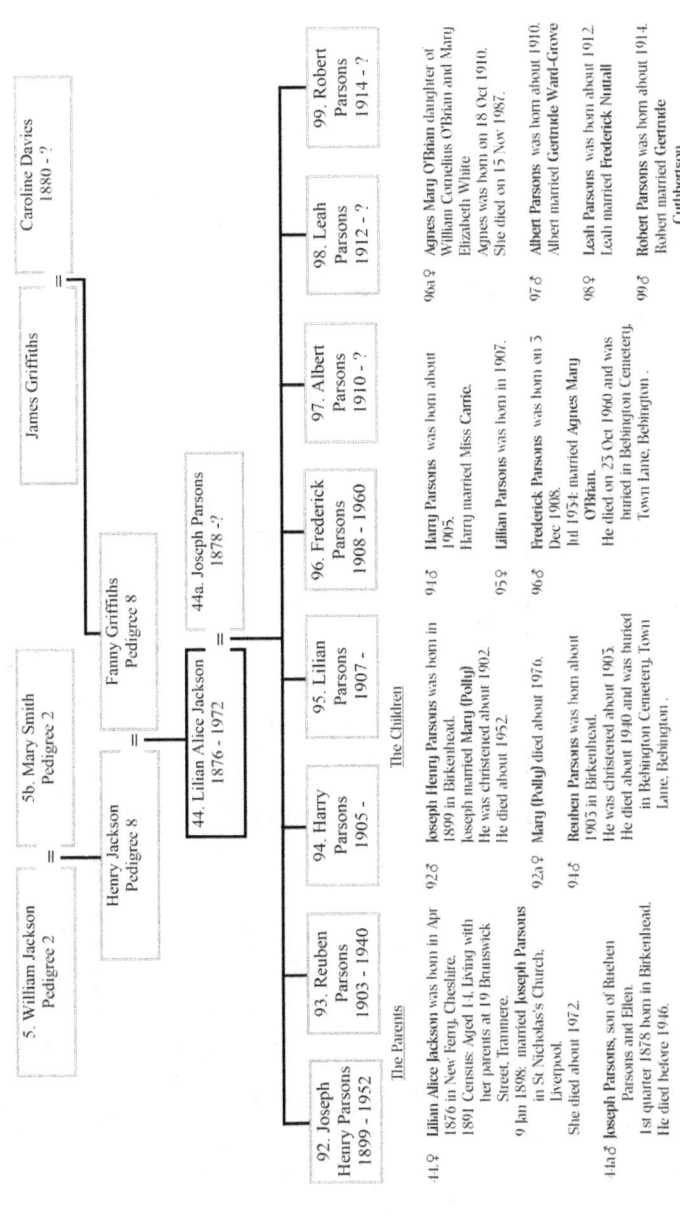

5. William Jackson
Pedigree 2

5b. Mary Smith
Pedigree 2

James Griffiths

Caroline Davies
1880 - ?

Henry Jackson
Pedigree 8

Fanny Griffiths
Pedigree 8

44. Lilian Alice Jackson
1876 - 1972

44a. Joseph Parsons
1878 -?

The Parents

| 92. Joseph Henry Parsons 1899 - 1952 | 93. Reuben Parsons 1903 - 1940 | 94. Harry Parsons 1905 - | 95. Lilian Parsons 1907 - | 96. Frederick Parsons 1908 - 1960 | 97. Albert Parsons 1910 - ? | 98. Leah Parsons 1912 - ? | 99. Robert Parsons 1914 - ? |

The Children

44.♀ **Lilian Alice Jackson** was born in Apr 1876 in New Ferry, Cheshire.
1891 Census: Aged 14. Living with her parents at 19 Brunswick Street, Tranmere.
9 Jan 1898: married **Joseph Parsons** in St Nicholas's Church, Liverpool.
She died about 1972.

44a.♂ **Joseph Parsons**, son of Rueben Parsons and Ellen.
1st quarter 1878 born in Birkenhead.
He died before 1946.

92.♂ **Joseph Henry Parsons** was born in 1899 in Birkenhead.
Joseph married **Mary (Polly)**.
He was christened about 1902.
He died about 1952.

93.♀ **Mary (Polly)** died about 1976.

93.♂ **Reuben Parsons** was born about 1903 in Birkenhead.
He was christened about 1903.
He died about 1940 and was buried in Bebington Cemetery, Town Lane, Bebington.

94.♂ **Harry Parsons** was born about 1905.
Harry married **Miss Carrie**.

95.♀ **Lilian Parsons** was born in 1907.

96.♂ **Frederick Parsons** was born on 5 Dec 1908.
In 1934 married **Agnes Mary O'Brian**.
He died on 23 Oct 1960 and was buried in Bebington Cemetery, Town Lane, Bebington .

96a.♀ **Agnes Mary O'Brian** daughter of William Cornelius O'Brian and Mary Elizabeth White
Agnes was born on 18 Oct 1910.
She died on 15 Nov 1987.

97.♂ **Albert Parsons** was born about 1910.
Albert married **Gertrude Ward-Grove**

98.♀ **Leah Parsons** was born about 1912.
Leah married **Frederick Nuttall**

99.♂ **Robert Parsons** was born about 1914.
Robert married **Gertrude Cuthbertson**.

Pedigree Nineteen
Lilian Alice Jackson 1876 - 1972

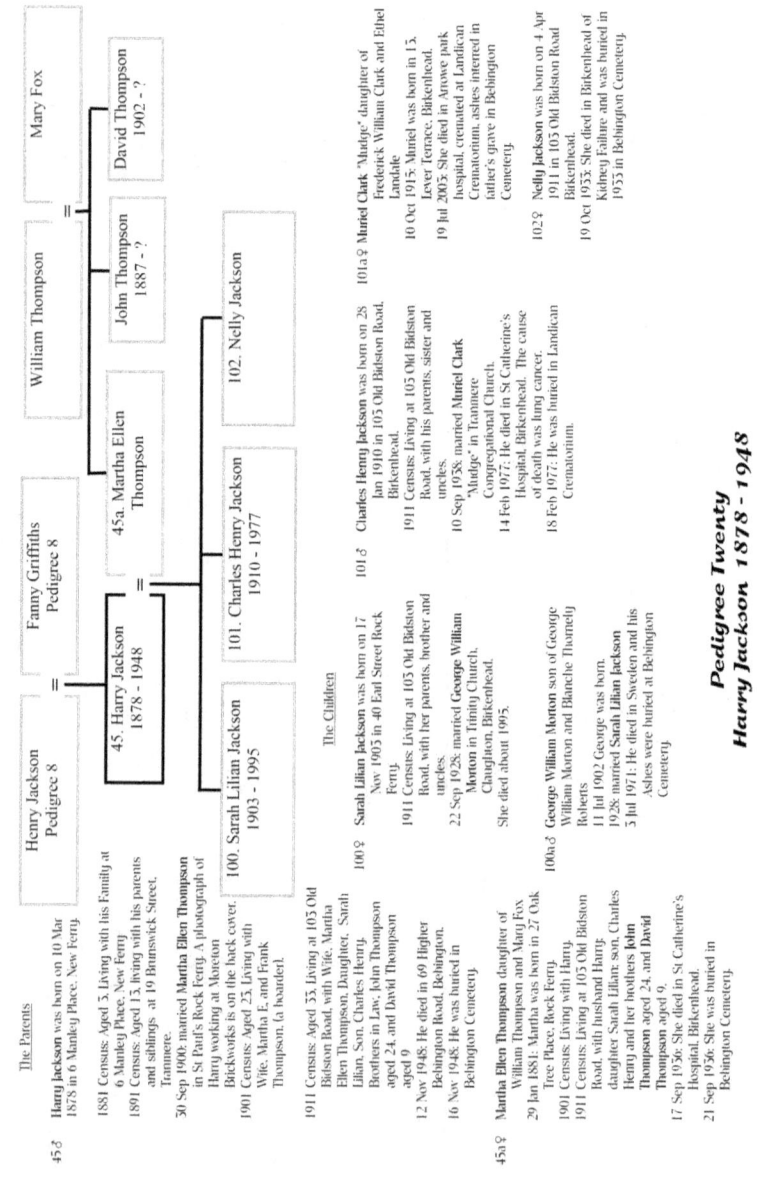

The Parents

Top boxes

Henry Jackson Pedigree 8 — Fanny Griffiths Pedigree 8 — William Thompson — Mary Fox

45. Harry Jackson 1878 - 1948 = 45a. Martha Ellen Thompson — John Thompson 1887 - ? — David Thompson 1902 - ?

100. Sarah Lilian Jackson 1903 - 1995 — 101. Charles Henry Jackson 1910 - 1977 — 102. Nelly Jackson

Parent details

45♂ Harry Jackson was born on 10 Mar 1878 in 6 Manley Place, New Ferry.
1881 Census: Aged 3, Living with his Family at 6 Manley Place, New Ferry
1891 Census: Aged 13, living with his parents and siblings at 19 Brunswick Street, Tranmere.
30 Sep 1900: married **Martha Ellen Thompson** in St Paul's Rock Ferry. A photograph of Harry working at Moreton Brickworks is on the back cover.
1901 Census: Aged 23 Living with Wife, Martha E, and Frank Thompson. (a boarder).
1911 Census: Aged 33, Living at 105 Old Bidston Road, with Wife, Martha Ellen Thompson, Daughter, Sarah Lilian, Son, Charles Henry, Brothers in Law, John Thompson aged 24, and David Thompson aged 9
12 Nov 1948: He died in 69 Higher Bebington Road, Bebington.
16 Nov 1948: He was buried in Bebington Cemetery

45a♀ Martha Ellen Thompson daughter of William Thompson and Mary Fox
29 Jan 1881: Martha was born in 27 Oak Tree Place, Rock Ferry.
1901 Census: Living with Harry
1911 Census: Living at 105 Old Bidston Road, with husband Harry, daughter Sarah Lilian, son, Charles Henry and her brothers **John Thompson** aged 24, and **David Thompson** aged 9.
17 Sep 1956: She died in St Catherine's Hospital, Birkenhead.
21 Sep 1956: She was buried in Bebington Cemetery.

The Children

100♀ Sarah Lilian Jackson was born on 17 Nov 1903 in 40 Eald Street Rock Ferry.
1911 Census: Living at 105 Old Bidston Road, with her parents, brother and uncles.
22 Sep 1928: married George William Morton in Trinity Church, Claughton, Birkenhead.
She died about 1995.

100a♂ George William Morton son of George William Morton and Blanche Thornely Roberts
11 Jul 1902: George was born.
1928: married **Sarah Lilian Jackson**
3 Jul 1971: He died in Sweeten and his Ashes were buried at Bebington Cemetery

101♂ Charles Henry Jackson was born on 28 Jan 1910 in 105 Old Bidston Road, Birkenhead.
1911 Census: Living at 105 Old Bidston Road, with his parents, sister and uncles.
10 Sep 1938: married Muriel Clark "Mudge" in Tranmere Congregational Church.
14 Feb 1977: He died in St Catherine's Hospital, Birkenhead. The cause of death was lung cancer.
18 Feb 1977: He was buried in Landican Crematorium.

101a♀ Muriel Clark "Mudge" daughter of Frederick William Clark and Ethel Landale
10 Oct 1915: Muriel was born in 13, Lever Terrace, Birkenhead.
19 Jul 2005: She died in Arowe park hospital, cremated at Landican Crematorium, ashes interred in father's grave in Bebington Cemetery

102♀ Nelly Jackson was born on 4 Apr 1911 in 105 Old Bidston Road Birkenhead.
19 Oct 1953: She died in Birkenhead of Kidney Failure and was buried in 1953 in Bebington Cemetery.

Pedigree Twenty
Harry Jackson 1878 - 1948

The Jackson Family at Trafalger Square *circa* 1947 :
Muriel (née Clark), Charles Henry, Colin (the author), Keith (with Gun)
See pedigree 20

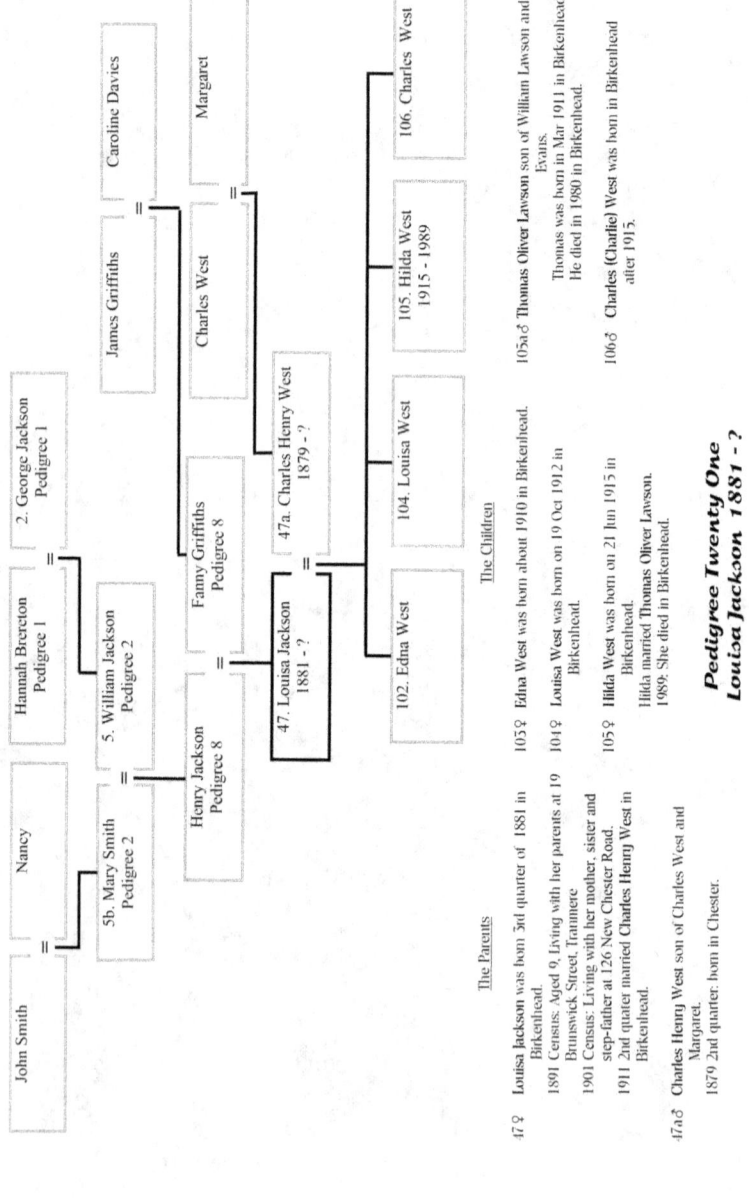

The Parents

47 ♀ **Louisa Jackson** was born 3rd quarter of 1881 in Birkenhead.
1891 Census: Aged 9. Living with her parents at 19 Brunswick Street, Tranmere.
1901 Census: Living with her mother, sister and step-father at 126 New Chester Road.
1911 2nd quarter married **Charles Henry West** in Birkenhead.

47a ♂ **Charles Henry West** son of Charles West and Margaret.
1879 2nd quarter: born in Chester.

The Children

105 ♀ **Edna West** was born about 1910 in Birkenhead.

104 ♀ **Louisa West** was born on 19 Oct 1912 in Birkenhead.

105 ♀ **Hilda West** was born on 21 Jun 1915 in Birkenhead.
Hilda married **Thomas Oliver Lawson**. 1989. She died in Birkenhead.

105a ♂ **Thomas Oliver Lawson** son of William Lawson and Evans.
Thomas was born in Mar 1911 in Birkenhead. He died in 1980 in Birkenhead.

106 ♂ **Charles (Charlie) West** was born in Birkenhead after 1915.

Pedigree Twenty One
Louisa Jackson 1881 - ?

www.ingramcontent.com/pod-product-compliance
Lightning Source LLC
Chambersburg PA
CBHW070845290526
45795CB00002B/995